YOU ARE THE BEST!

REAL LOVE

I LOVE YOU

XOXO

CUTIE PIE

CUP CAKE

FEBRUARY

SWEET PEA

YOU AND ME

I LOVE YOU

HUG ME

ALL MINE

BE TRUE

SUN SHINE!

ONE I LOVE

YOU'RE SWEET

Thank you for your recent purchase! We hope you've enjoyed your Valentine Coloring Card.
Happy Valentine's Day!
From florabella publishing

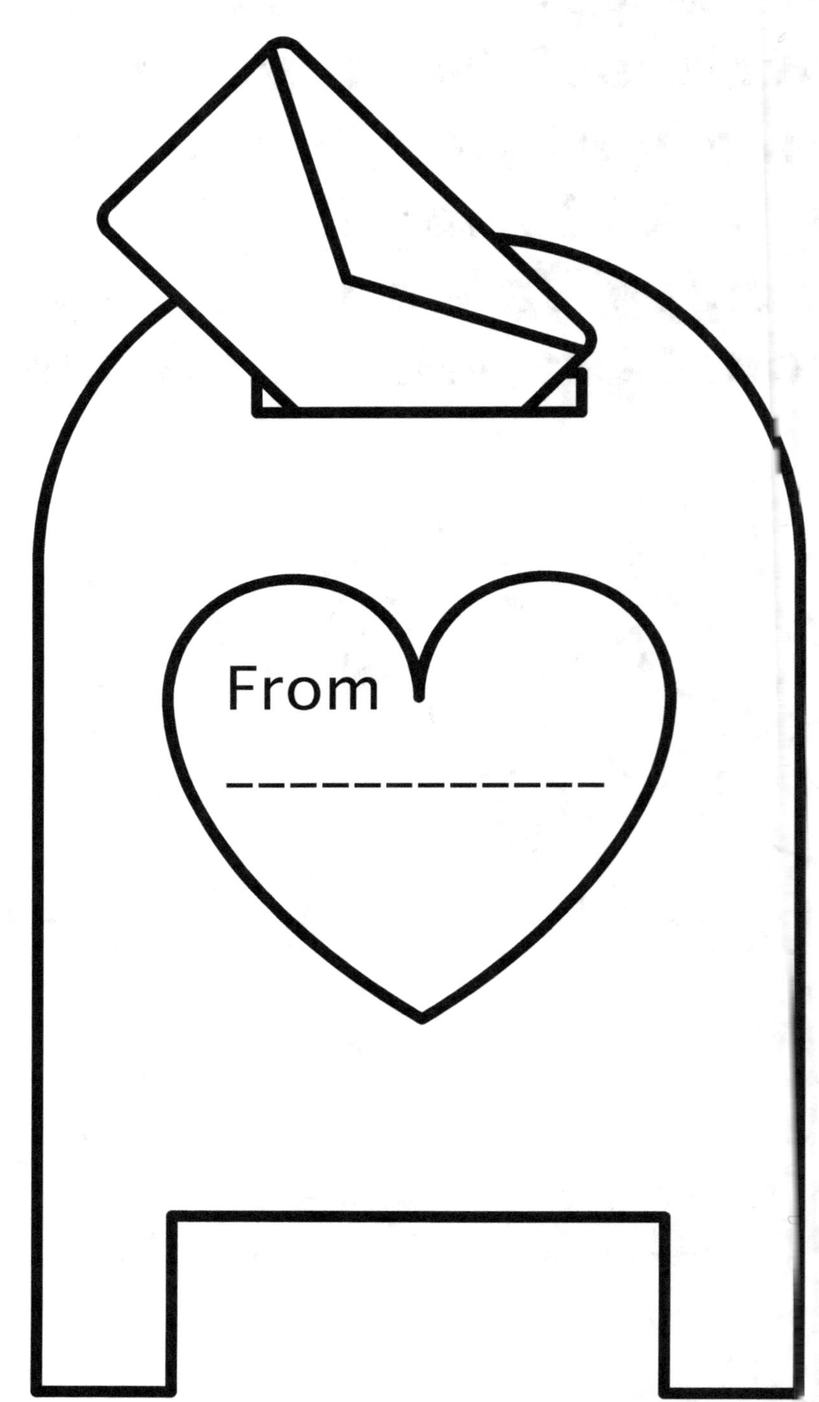
From

www.ingramcontent.com/pod-product-compliance
Lightning Source LLC
Chambersburg PA
CBHW050711250726
48662CB00002B/968